IMAGES
*of America*

# ROXBOROUGH

IMAGES
*of America*

# ROXBOROUGH

Deborah Del Collo for the
Roxborough, Manayunk, and Wissahickon
Historical Society

ARCADIA
PUBLISHING

Published by Arcadia Publishing
Charleston, South Carolina

Library of Congress Control Number: 2010942701

For all general information, please contact Arcadia Publishing:
Telephone 843-853-2070
Fax 843-853-0044
E-mail sales@arcadiapublishing.com
For customer service and orders:
Toll-Free 1-888-313-2665

Visit us on the Internet at www.arcadiapublishing.com

*To Sylvia Myers and the late Nick Myers for their inspiring
enthusiasm and dedication to Roxborough's past.*

# CONTENTS

# ACKNOWLEDGMENTS

First and foremost, this book could not have come about without the tireless efforts of two people, Sylvia Myers and John Johnstone. They shared their abundance of knowledge and resources of Roxborough without fail. The Roxborough, Manayunk, and Wissahickon Historical Society (RMWHS) is such an important entity in the community, and its members should be proud to have such an organization that promotes its history in many ways.

I would like to thank the following other residents, past and present, who have helped with the creation of this publication over the last year: Harry Garforth, Donald Sloan, John Hartman, John Kiker, Judy Jones, Nick Bucci, and Donna Howley.

Thank you to the Roxborough Development Corporation and the *Review* for your community support.

I would also like to acknowledge the excellent help from our editor Erin Vosgien, who was always just an e-mail away.

And finally I'd like to thank my colleagues, family, and friends, at work and home, who have supported me through this process.

# INTRODUCTION

Roxborough, also known as the 21st Ward of Philadelphia, is a community of many Philadelphia firsts. Although established in 1690, its origins and development date to many years before that.

The first explorers and settlers in the area found the native speakers of the Lenni Lenape language, which is a dialect of expressions based mostly on nature. The spelling of Lenape words differs somewhat in the English language. The words *manatawney* and *manaiung* are intertwined with the beginnings of Roxborough. The Manatawney, which is currently Ridge Avenue in Roxborough, is a path from the native plantations of upper Roxborough to the Falls of Schuylkill in the current East Falls section of Roxborough. The Manaiung is the part of the Schuylkill River that borders the land of Roxborough. The combination of *mana* or *mona* (raging, god, or creation) and *tawney* (open road) in Ridge Avenue's original Lenape name Manatawney roughly means "an open road from our creator." The addition of *iung* (water or river) to mana in Manaiung translates to a "raging river," which makes perfect sense since the waters of the Schuylkill bordering Roxborough were raging waters in Lenape days. The Wissahickon is a creek that passes through the middle and southeast end of Roxborough. *Wisa* can mean "catfish" or "yellow," and *hickon* means "mouth of a stream or tide;" therefore, Wissahickon likely means "a large catch of catfish found at the mouth of the creek."

In 1623, Dutch explorers from New Amsterdam (New York City) traveled upstream on the Delaware River and noticed they had passed the mouth of a river obscured by trees, which would only have been noticed otherwise while traveling downstream. They named it Schuylkill, meaning "hidden river." They eventually traveled the Schuylkill upstream and could only go a few miles before they came upon falls, causing them to go no further. They named them the Falls of Schuylkill. At those falls was a plentiful fishing hole and a native footpath leading northwest along a ridge, between valleys of the Schuylkill River and the nearby Wissahickon Creek. At the Falls of Schuylkill, a trading post was established between Lenni Lenape natives and the Dutch. The Dutch not only established a community (Falls of Schuylkill) but also guarded the Schuylkill River from British explorers from the south. It is likely that at those falls, the first interaction between a Dutch explorer and a native occurred within the current boundaries of Philadelphia, thus establishing the first trading post in Philadelphia.

Other than the Manatawney, the only other major road was a native trail that began at the Delaware River near Chester, Pennsylvania, passed through Merion, traversed over the Schuylkill via a rope bridge, and continued where the current Wigard Avenue is in Roxborough. It then traveled to the Summit, intersected Ridge Avenue, went through Chestnut Hill, and crossed into Bucks County. The Summit is the highest point not only in Roxborough but also in Philadelphia. An 1848 Roxborough map shows what was left of the trail, listed as the "Old Road," in the location of the current Wigard Avenue. It is believed that William Penn, with the help of local natives, traveled this road upon his first visit to the Roxborough tracts in 1682.

It was not long before the Dutch settled into the Falls of Schuylkill and along the Wissahickon

Creek. As early as 1654, Swedes settled into areas upstream along the Schuylkill River and established fisheries and farmsteads at the north end of current Manayunk, near the Schuylkill River. Their village's name was Cinnaminson; an adjoining community, which consisted of a group of Swedish blockhouses, one of which still exists in Manayunk, was called the Blocks.

By 1682, William Penn established German Township, which was composed of the current areas of Roxborough, Germantown, Mount Airy, and Chestnut Hill. Although 11 tracts of land within German Township would eventually become Roxborough Township, those tracts were not yet isolated from the other land parcels in German Township. The 11 land tracts that eventually made up Roxborough all bordered the Schuylkill River. The first landowners of those tracts were mostly British businessmen sent by William Penn. They built mills along the Wissahickon Creek and took over plantations surrounding Ridge Avenue, which were previously farmed by the Lenni Lenape, the Dutch, and the Swedes. The Roxborough area became industrial, and in 1687, the Ridge Road, ending at current Barren Hill, was expanded north to the Plymouth Limekilns, on the current Germantown Pike. Goods were transported on Ridge Avenue to the Falls of Schuylkill, where they would then travel downstream by boat to Philadelphia. Falls of Schuylkill was eventually renamed Fort Saint David, after a Welsh saint, popularized by Philadelphia's prominent businessmen, who vacationed there and thought the area had the best fishing and most comfortable tavern accommodations.

A Mennonite minister from Germany named William Rittenhouse moved onto land at the northeast corner of what was to become Roxborough Township, along the Monoshone Creek, in 1688. He performed the first baptisms in Philadelphia at that creek and established the first paper mill in America in 1690, with the help of William Bradford, a printer. He was also the great-grandfather of David Rittenhouse, a famous mathematician, astronomer, and inventor, born in Roxborough Township in 1732 at the Rittenhouse Homestead. Besides being an independent, industrial community, it was the only paper manufacturer in America for 40 years. The site is currently the Historic Rittenhouse Town and is in the National Register of Historic Places and retains early Rittenhouse homes.

In 1690, the chief justice for Pennsylvania, Andrew Robeson, established a township boundary for Roxborough, which consisted of 11 tracts of land, separating it from the prior German Township—only the chief justice was entitled to establish a township boundary. It is believed by some historians that the boundary was created because of the rapid industrial growth that was occurring in Roxborough, with mills, plantations, fisheries, and construction. In 1690, Robeson purchased the land tract comprising Falls of Schuylkill and built the first estate house along Ridge Avenue. The surrounding grounds were then known as Shoomac Park, named for the many Sumac trees in the area. Robeson was from Kelso, Roxborough, Scotland, and named his newly built house and property the Roxborough estate. Robeson passed away in 1694, and his nephew, also named Andrew, became chief justice and eventually took over the estate. Although the Robesons were Scottish, they were members of Swedes Church in Philadelphia. The Robesons remained at the Roxborough estate through the 1850s.

In 1691, two brothers from Germany, Wigard and Gerhard Levering, established a business district for Roxborough along Ridge Avenue at the center of the township. It was named Levering's Town or Leverington, and today, the Leverington Cemetery and Leverington Presbyterian Church retain the original name. The Leverings were responsible for much of the early stone construction in Roxborough and Manayunk and established the first schoolhouse in Roxborough. Local Baptists in Leverington organized the first Baptist church in Roxborough in 1789.

William Penn encouraged those in Europe who sought religious freedom to come to Pennsylvania. Of particular interest was Johannes Kelpius, a scholar, musician, and educator, who came to settle in the wilderness of Roxborough in 1694. He was born in Transylvania, Romania. Kelpius became a famous writer and the leader of the "Ridge Hermits" or "Mystics of the Wissahickon," a group of men who resided in the woods surrounding the Wissahickon Creek and had a tabernacle of worship. Many believed that the mystics had powers and would bring their children and animals to be healed by them. One of the mystics, Dr. Christopher Witt, painted the first oil painting in

America of Johannes Kelpius, which is now at the Pennsylvania Historical Society. The Ridge Hermits are also known as the first American cult.

Roxborough Township saw a rapid industrial growth with the expansion of the Ridge Road. In 1707, it extended southeast to Center City Philadelphia at the corner of High Street (currently Market Street). To the northwest, it expanded to the Perkiomen Creek. Until 1760, Ridge Road took the route of the current Germantown Pike, from Church Road in Lafayette Hill, through Plymouth and Norriton, to the Perkiomen Creek. It was further extended to Reading, Pennsylvania, by 1720 and was called the "Great Road from Philadelphia to Reading" or the "King's Road." With this industrial growth of Roxborough, the Wissahickon Valley and Creek, previously thought of as a paradise, were no longer inhabitable for the Lenni Lenape natives, as their natural habitat was littered with industrial waste. Some natives moved west and some stayed, mixing with Caucasian or African American families throughout Philadelphia. In 1760, Ridge Avenue took its current route through Norristown and Perkiomenville, continuing to Reading. Mile markers, also known as milestones, were placed along the road. The ninth milestone still remains in Roxborough and is found at the corner of Ridge and Port Royal (previously Ship Lane) Avenues.

By 1775, Roxborough Township featured many independent, industrial communities. Col. Henry Hill, under George Washington, organized the Roxborough Regiment and began training soldiers for the upcoming Revolutionary War. Soldiers enlisted in the regiment at Fort Saint David, near Henry Hill's home. By 1776, over 90 Roxborough men had joined the fight for independence from the British. Though there were only a few skirmishes in Roxborough during the Revolution, the majority of casualties occurred in the nearby Battle of Germantown. Many soldiers from neighboring states were encamped in Roxborough during the summer and fall of 1777. George Washington stayed at Henry Hill's house on Queen Lane in August 1777. Approximately 11,000 soldiers were present in Roxborough after the Battle of Brandywine and prior to their walk to the Valley Forge encampment in November 1777. They walked down a snow-covered Ship Lane in Roxborough, currently Port Royal Avenue, en route to Valley Forge for training.

Following the victory of the American Revolution, land previously governed by the British was sold into smaller plots, and the building of homes, farms, and mills increased in Roxborough Township. The primary building material was Wissahickon schist, a rock found only in the Wissahickon Valley. It is a pliable rock that expands and contracts with the seasons and can only be found in communities surrounding the Wissahickon Valley, making buildings in the area unique. As the community developed, the Ridge Road became heavily used and was in constant need of repair. In 1811, the Ridge Road was paved (laid with Belgian block) and became the Ridge Turnpike, with tollbooths extending from Philadelphia to Perkiomenville, which were in use until 1870.

With anthracite coal being discovered in Pennsylvania's coal regions, the Schuylkill Navigation Company was formed to develop a river/canal system to safely transport coal and other goods 94 miles from Port Clinton, Pennsylvania, to Philadelphia. The first boat to carry coal on the waterway was in 1825. The transport of coal and the convenience of the waterway greatly impacted the region. Immigrants came from Great Britain to build and open mills in Manayunk along the navigable waterway. Manayunk, between 1810 and 1825, was referred to as "Flat Rock," due to the presence of flat rocks in the nearby river. Manayunk became a borough within Roxborough Township in 1825. It soon became the largest industrial area in the Philadelphia region.

The Philadelphia, Germantown & Norristown Railroad started passenger service from Ninth and Green Streets in Philadelphia to Germantown. A branch extending to Norristown was completed in the spring of 1835, with service arriving in Manayunk during the fall of 1834. That line is still in operation; however, the station names and locations were somewhat different. The stations looked more like taverns or country homes. Within the boundaries of Roxborough Township, the trains stopped at School House Lane, Wissahickon, Manayunk, Springfield (where Ivy Ridge Station is), Green Tree (currently Shawmont), and Princeton (near Miquon). The trains were mostly horse-drawn until several locomotives were purchased in 1836. Today's Shawmont Station is the only remaining original station on that line and is in the Philadelphia

Register of Historic Places as the oldest passenger railway station in the United States. In 1874, the Ridge Avenue and Barren Hill Trolley Company ran horse-drawn trolleys from Center City Philadelphia on the Ridge Road to Barren Hill, just past the Roxborough boundary. The trolleys became electrified in 1894 and ran until the 1940s.

By 1842, the Philadelphia and Reading Railroad (P&R) completed a line from Broad and Cherry Streets in Philadelphia to Pottsville, Pennsylvania, running on the opposite side of the Schuylkill River. It also built the Port Richmond branch, which crossed the Schuylkill in East Falls and was used for trains to transport coal to the Delaware River. The Schuylkill Navigation Company lost revenue to the railroad, due to the railroad's ability to transport coal to Philadelphia in five hours as compared to a boat's six-day trip. The Reading Railroad took over the Philadelphia, Germantown & Norristown Railroad, along with the Schuylkill Navigation Company, in 1870. They also built the Venice branch for transport of goods from mills along the Manayunk Canal. The last boats to carry freight along the Schuylkill River were in 1916.

As Manayunk thrived industrially through the latter half of the 19th century and immigrants came from Europe to work in its mills, the Wissahickon Valley became recognized for its beauty as a natural area. The Fairmount Park Commission was formed, leading to the closure of mills along the Wissahickon Creek. Hotels opened along the creek in the mid-19th century, and eventually, nature reclaimed much of the damage to the area caused by industry during post-Colonial times. In the 20th century, the Great Depression caused several Manayunk Mills to close, and industrial development came to a halt there.

Today, communities within the original boundaries of Roxborough Township are thriving with culture, art, and natural beauty. The Wissahickon Valley is recognized as one of the most beautiful places in the world, with hiking, biking, and equestrian trails, with many visitors from foreign places. Manayunk has become a mecca for arts and fashion, and the industrial buildings there have been transformed into businesses and residences. The most difficult bike race in the world runs through Manayunk. The Schuylkill Valley Nature Center in Roxborough houses a large environmental and wildlife education center. Building owners and local historians are placing historic buildings in the local register of historic places as well as the National Register. As much as the area has been transformed, there is still much recognition, funding, and work needed to preserve what remains in the community from olden times. Many structures unique to Roxborough have been recently demolished, including several stone houses over 200 years old and one-of-a-kind buildings unique to the area, causing new construction to overshadow historic structures and to obscure natural areas.

Many early families with their cultural traditions originated in Roxborough. My sole purpose in writing this introduction is to bring about preservation, recognition, and appreciation to a historic community.

—John Johnstone, Roxborough resident and past-president,
Roxborough, Manayunk, and Wissahickon Historical Society

# One

# FIRST, OLDEST, AND ONE OF A KIND

Currently known as Glen Fern, the Thomas Livezey estate became part of Fairmount Park in 1869. This 1.5-story center section of the estate is said to have been built during the first German occupation in German Township during the 1680s, but lacking records on this section, there is a possibility that it was built during an earlier Dutch occupation in Roxborough. Its construction is very similar to the original section of the Wyckoff House in Brooklyn, New York, built in 1652. According to the Livezey family, the center section was present in 1685, its kitchen was added in 1696, and the main house was constructed in 1732, with an expansion in 1745. (Courtesy of John Johnstone.)

Inside the oldest section of the Glen Fern estate is a large closable hearth fireplace. The floor was dirt when this photograph was taken in 1909. (Courtesy of Eric Sabaroff / Valley Green Canoe Club.)

A winter's day in 1917 displays the natural beauty of the snowy woods combined with the Wissahickon schist construction of Glen Fern. A large estate, with sections ascending from large to small, is classified architecturally as telescoping construction. (Courtesy of Eric Sabaroff /Valley Green Canoe Club.)

Pictured in front of Glen Fern in 1915, Gorgas W. Bechtel, the head of the Valley Green Canoe Club, is surrounded by Mary Riley (left) and Kathryn Ritter. (Courtesy of Eric Sabaroff / Valley Green Canoe Club.)

Little is known of the very first owners of this c. 1680 residence at 900 Northwestern Ave. The original section of the house was a 12-by-15-foot log building with a short stone foundation and a stone fireplace with a wooden lintel. It was later enlarged but retains the original small foundation and ancient fireplace. The wooden lintel in the fireplace, as opposed to stone, indicates lack of manpower and a very early, isolated settlement. Not only is it the oldest permanent residence in Roxborough but also the oldest in all of Philadelphia, predating William Penn's first visit. (Courtesy of the Philadelphia Historical Commission.)

Also at 900 Northwestern Ave. is the oldest barn in Philadelphia, dating to 1690. It is a German forebay barn, with ground entrances at two levels; the upper is used to facilitate smaller, lighter animals and feed, and the lower is for larger, heavier animals. There are only slits in the mortar for limited light, as an animal could knock out windows. (Courtesy of the Philadelphia Historical Commission.)

This c. 1690 outdoor root cellar at 900 Northwestern Ave. was used primarily for fall storage of pumpkins and gourds that were used to feed livestock in the nearby barn during the winter. (Courtesy of David Rowan.)

Built in 1690 by Philadelphia Swedes, this house belonged to Pennsylvania chief justice Andrew Robeson. It was the first estate house along Ridge Avenue within the grounds of Shoomac Park. This house is associated with one of earliest gristmills in Pennsylvania. (Courtesy of phillyhistory.org, a project of the Philadelphia Department of Records.)

Standing at the head of the Wissahickon Valley, Robeson's estate commanded an important crossroads for travelers and waggoners. Its mill site, with its accessible location, entered into Gen. George Washington's plan of attack on Germantown. Here is Robeson's Roxborough estate house along Ridge Avenue as depicted in a 1913 John G. Bullock lantern slide of an early-1700s sketch. (Courtesy of The Library Company of Pennsylvania.)

SHALL
the Magnificent

WISSAHICKON
VALLEY

1684                    1760

AND THE ANCIENT SHOOMAC
MANSION

BE
DESTROYED?

WRITE TO YOUR COUNCILMAN
NOW

PROTEST
NOW OR NEVER!

Concerned residents tried to save the Robeson estate house. It survived until 1961, when the City Avenue Bridge off-ramp construction required its demolition. (Courtesy of Nick Bucci.)

The 1690 stone home of William Rittenhouse sits along the Monoshone Creek in the northeast corner of Roxborough Township. William Rittenhouse performed Philadelphia's first baptisms at this site and also opened America's first paper mill here. The house became a bake house, used to keep cooking soot out of the home, when another house was built nearby in 1707. It currently has a large hearth fireplace with an upper loft. (Courtesy of John Johnstone.)

The left half of this house was built in 1707, and the right half was built in 1713. In 1732, it was the birthplace of David Rittenhouse, a famous inventor and astronomer, for whom Philadelphia's Rittenhouse Square is named. This house is the heart of Historic Rittenhouse Town. (Courtesy of John Johnstone.)

A drawing, copied from America's oldest oil painting by Dr. Christopher Witt, depicts Johannes Kelpius, of the Ridge Hermits or Mystics of the Wissahickon, as he would have appeared over 300 years ago. The original painting is located at the Historical Society of Pennsylvania. Kelpius's life remains to this day shrouded in an air of mystery and romance. The Kelpius Society of Roxborough strives to document and educate. (Courtesy of Sylvia Myers.)

This 1690s outdoor root cellar was originally used to store feed for livestock; later, it became a place of meditation for Johannes Kelpius until his death in 1708. It is currently deep within the woods of Wissahickon Park. (Courtesy of Sylvia Myers.)

At right below, 7549 Ridge Ave. was built in 1717, and 7551 Ridge Ave. (left side) was added on in 1784. The right side of the building was the center for a large flax plantation with a linseed oil mill behind it. The mill was located along a stream, called Oil Mill Run. Though it was originally built for Thomas Storey, a Quaker minister, it was occupied and run by the Livezey family from 1717 until 1788. Rex family members resided there until 1852 and used the barn for their blacksmith business. It is currently the oldest house on Ridge Avenue between Philadelphia and Reading. (Courtesy of John Johnstone.)

An early German artisan who was a palatine (a person possessing royal privileges) from the Black Forest carved this oak leaf, with bordering shelves and stonework, at the old 7549 Ridge Ave. house. Such crafts are unusual for a house built in 1717, and there are no others like this or as old in Philadelphia. Similar carvings are found on cuckoo clocks. (Courtesy of John Johnstone.)

As early as 1654, Swedes settled into nearby areas along creeks and rivers and established farms and fisheries. On the north end of current Manayunk in the 4800 block of Ogle Street remains the last of three Swedish blockhouses, which used to be found in abundance in the small village of Blocks, bordering a section of Roxborough named Cinnaminson. This house has a Swedish gambrel roof. It was once four residences within a square. This c. 1720 house predates the borough of Manayunk, within Roxborough Township. It is the only building of its type left in Philadelphia and the oldest house in current Manayunk. (Courtesy of John Johnstone.)

Most historians believe that the Valley Green Inn was built in 1855, which is true, but only the wood-framed section (right side) was added to an existing stone house at that time. The left side of the building shows a classic early Wissahickon schist home of the area, with 18-inch stone walls and small rooms, dating to the 1700s. It is the last remaining inn along the Wissahickon Creek in Roxborough that still serves food. (Courtesy of the RMWHS.)

This yellow-painted schoolhouse, built in 1810, is currently the oldest one-room schoolhouse in Philadelphia. Dormer windows were added to the second floor when it became a residence in the 1940s. At Wises Mill Road and Shawmont Avenue, it is now painted white. (Courtesy of the RMWHS.)

Shawmont Station is currently the oldest passenger railway station in the United States, dating to 1834. Up until 1873, it was called "Green Tree," named for nearby Green Tree Run. It received a small rear addition and Victorian upgrades in 1870. Pictured in 1929, it had a small freight station at that time as well. (Courtesy of the Reading Railroad Historical Society.)

Passing by Shawmont Station is Reading Railroad's express to Reading, Tamaqua, and Shamokin in 1948. (Courtesy of the Reading Railroad Historical Society.)

Engine 66 is Upper Roxborough's old fire station dating to 1864 and sits beside the old Dearnley Park reservoir. It currently is used for a construction business and is at Dearnley Avenue and Eva Street. (Courtesy of the Fire Museum of Philadelphia.)

Before being demolished for new construction in 2004, despite local attempts to save it, the Joseph Dearnley mansion was a rare Victorian marvel, built by architects Hales and Ballinger in 1897. They built famous religious and commercial buildings in Philadelphia. It featured Italianate, Chateau-esque, and Gothic-Tudor architecture styles and was constructed with local stone. Its entrance was at Flamingo and Silverwood Streets, and its land is now occupied with modern, "cookie-cutter" construction. (Courtesy of John Johnstone.)

This c. 1850 barn, presently at 6822 Ridge Avenue, was the first barn in which famous helicopter inventor and pioneer, Joseph Piasecki, worked to develop America's first useful helicopter in 1936. He also started the "P-V Engineering Forum," with a group of engineering students from the University of Pennsylvania, which he attended. (Courtesy of John Johnstone.)

In 1940, helicopter inventor Frank Piasecki used this second, larger building, located across from the intersection of Ridge and Fairthorne Avenues. This artwork depicts the unveiling of his aircraft, which he finished developing at this site, the "PV-2" in 1943. It was the second helicopter invented in America and considered the first useful one, setting the standards for future helicopters. (Courtesy of the RMWHS.)

Frank Piasecki tests his early PV-2 aircraft in 1943. The helicopter was towed by car or truck to a local baseball field at night so as not to disrupt traffic on Livezy Lane. The workers' headlights supplied the light. (Courtesy of Francis J. Bell.)

Crockery was common in German and Roxborough Townships during Colonial times, used primarily for pickling as a preservative. The painted patterns are typical of early German settlers. (Courtesy of Wesley Cording.)

A common dishware during Colonial times was pewter, but it is no longer considered safe to use due to its lead content. (Courtesy of Wesley Cording.)

Fireplaces were not only used for heating the home during Colonial times but also for cooking meals. Handles were long on frying pans to prevent burns. (Courtesy of Wesley Cording.)

A Revolutionary War musket, found in the attic of a log cabin in Roxborough, now adorns this Colonial fireplace. Also pictured are some plates with Native American designs. (Courtesy of Wesley Cording.)

Pewter spirit measurers were used in taverns during Colonial times to assure that patrons got what they were paying for. These came from the Roxboro Tavern, which stood at Ridge Avenue and Domino Lane. (Courtesy of Wesley Cording.)

# Two

# ALONG THE RIDGE

The Old Falls Tavern was built in 1731 as the Saint David's Hotel, where Philadelphia's elite would meet during vacation at Fort Saint David. Vacationers fished at nearby falls during Colonial times. With the development of mills in Manayunk and subsequent pollution of the Schuylkill River, the vacation spot ceased to attract visitors. The Old Falls Tavern was demolished in 1971. (Courtesy of the Philadelphia Historical Commission.)

This house at 4414 Ridge Ave., built in 1789, was the property of Peter and Jonathan Robeson. They were descendents of Andrew Robeson, who had built an estate house across the street from this one. The house was demolished in 1997 after being on Ridge Avenue in East Falls for 208 years. (Courtesy of the Philadelphia Historical Commission.)

Prior to the 1920s, this site along Ridge Avenue near Rochelle Avenue was the Wissahickon Café. (Courtesy of John Kiker.)

Morrison's Drugstore was in operation for many years on Ridge Avenue. Local bottle makers bottled Morrison family remedies, marked with the pharmacy's name, and those antique bottles can still be found in the area. (Courtesy of John Kiker.)

Only a small retaining wall exists today from this 1726 house built by Peter Righter where Ridge Avenue and Righter Street meet. During the American Revolution, it was a hospital. It became the Plow Tavern in 1802, a "poor house" in 1833, and was demolished in 1937. The Righters were famous for "Righter's Ferry," a combination rope/boat ferry crossing the Schuylkill River into Bala Cynwyd. (Courtesy of Saint Timothy's Episcopal Church.)

The 1850 Barnes house at the intersection of Ridge Avenue, Righter Street, and Hermit Street is an unusual combination of late Federal and ornate Victorian, constructed of Wissahickon schist. It currently adorns this busy corner. (Courtesy of James Barnes.)

Cows graze in Harry and Susan Root's pasture on Righter Street, just below Hermit Street, where the present-day Cook-Wissahickon School is located. (Courtesy of Grace and James Barnes.)

A stone date plate of 1743 adorns this large Colonial home at 5513 Ridge Ave. Unfortunately, this house was recently demolished. (Courtesy of the Philadelphia Historical Commission.)

5513 Rear Side View

THE OLD WOODS BARN (1750)
Formerly Used as a Church by Grace Congregation
Roxborough, Phila.

Andrew Wood's barn was the site of a massacre in December 1777, when the English slaughtered 18 Virginian patriots seeking shelter. A memorial in Leverington Cemetery is in place for those patriots. (Courtesy of the RMWHS.)

The Colonial Andrew Wood estate, adjacent to Wood's barn, stood at Ridge and Roxborough Avenues. Pictured are Grace Lutheran congregation members on July 4, 1906. (Courtesy of Judy Jones.)

The Wood house was demolished in 1909. This photograph shows the workers on the left porch roof. (Courtesy of Judy Jones.)

Most homes in Roxborough were built of the local Wissahickon schist, but this one, built in 1895, is of granite and copper, the most expensive building materials of its day. This was the Langhurst estate and was last occupied in 1972. It is currently owned by Intercommunity Action Inc., or "Interac," and displays Gothic-Tudor architecture. (Courtesy of the Philadelphia Historical Commission.)

Near the site of a current diner at Ridge and Lyceum Avenues is Lyceum Hall, pictured in the 1890s. Lyceum Hall served as an office building, school, and library prior to its demolition following a 1966 fire. (Courtesy of the RMWHS.)

The Leverington Hotel, pictured during the 1880s, stood at the corner of Ridge and Leverington Avenues. The first hotel was smaller and built in 1731. George Washington referred to it as "Levrin's Tavern." It caught fire in 1783 and was rebuilt the following year. (Courtesy of the RMWHS.)

In the 1890s, cupolas were added to bring the hotel up to date. It was demolished in 1928 before the construction of the long-gone Roxy Theater. Its original date stone was saved and is in front of the Roxborough Library at Ridge Avenue and Hermitage Streets. (Courtesy of Trudy Smith.)

At the corner of Ridge and Leverington Avenues, the Leverington Hotel stood from 1731 to 1928. The Roxy Theater took its place and remained in operation until 1979. Before its fire and demolition in 1982, it briefly served as a concert hall and a skateboard rink. A small part of the original building facade can still be seen above what is now Dunkin' Donuts. (Courtesy of James Lamont.)

The Roxy Theater operated as a popular movie venue, as pictured prior to 1960. Even in the 1970s, weekend matinees were 50¢ and featured black and white "B" horror movies. (Courtesy of John Kiker.)

This house was built in 1796 and belonged to Col. Aaron Levering, who served in the American Revolution. Horatio Gates-Jones later purchased it and opened it as the Hotel George Washington. It became the first meeting place for the Roxborough Masonic Lodge in 1813. This house still stands at 6341 Ridge Ave. Its stable, which has been converted to a home, is also still behind the house. The porch was removed when Ridge Avenue was widened. (Courtesy of the Philadelphia Historical Commission.)

Gorgas Park, pictured in the 1950s before the monument was built, was a great place to ramble. The park land was donated to the city by Susan Gorgas. (Courtesy of RMWHS.)

RIDGE AVE

6237 and 6239 Ridge Ave. appear to be twin homes, but 6237 (right side) was built in 1740, and 6239 (left side) was added in the 20th century. There were many small houses similar to 6237 with storefront windows from Colonial times, but most survivors have been altered so as not to be easily distinguished as Colonial. This pair was demolished in 1999. (Courtesy of the Philadelphia Historical Commission.)

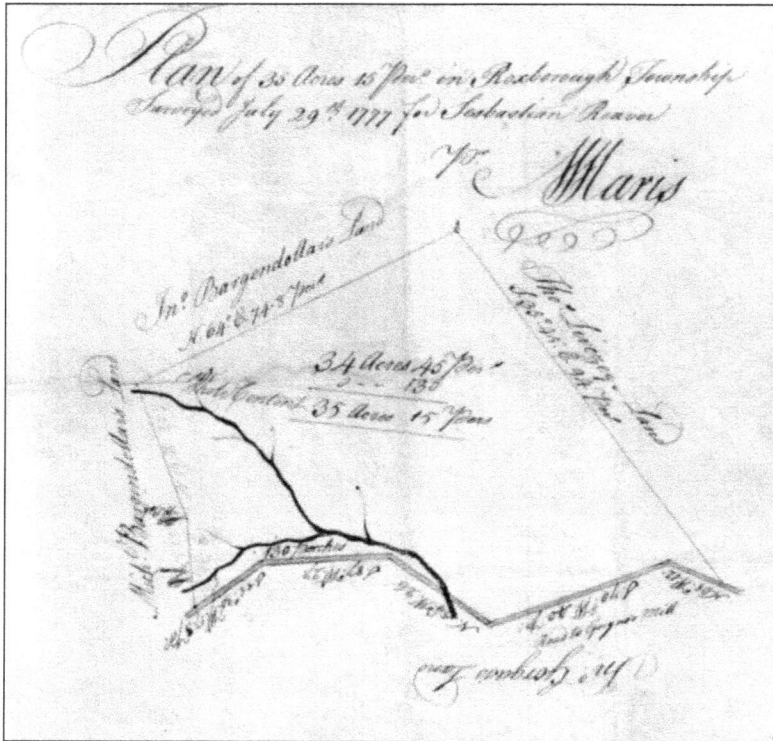

This is a 1777 pocket map that depicts the Bergendehler and Gorgas properties. The map, however, lacks Ridge Avenue as its central road. Likely, this was used by a Continental soldier during the American Revolution to identify the area without giving a specific location in the event of capture by the British. (Courtesy of Wesley Cording.)

6533 and 6535 Ridge Ave. were once a general and hardware store in 1800. It remains mostly unchanged from its Wissahickon schist facade and ornamental glasswork above its doors. After the store closed, it was divided into two residences. (Courtesy of the Philadelphia Historical Commission.)

The Roxy Drug Store at the southwest corner of Ridge and Leverington Avenues was the primary drug store in Roxborough's Business District for one hundred years. It was established in the days when a pharmacist was qualified to make his own drugs and stitch an open wound by request. It is currently a popular luncheon. (Courtesy of RMWHS.)

The old Lafayette Hotel at 6835 Ridge Ave., now a funeral home, was built in 1788. Its open porch is now enclosed, but upon entering, its doorways are of fine leaded glasswork that was classic of Philadelphia's Federal period. It has key-stoned woodwork throughout, which is also from the Federal period. (Courtesy of the Philadelphia Historical Commission.)

Found at 6926 Ridge Ave., this house was built by Christopher Ozias in 1825 and had random Ashlar mason work combined with Wissahickon Schist. It was placed in the Philadelphia Register of Historic Places but fell into disrepair, and the owner had it demolished in 2008, unbeknownst to the historical commission. It has been replaced with a bank. (Courtesy of the Philadelphia Historical Commission.)

The Starnes of Roxborough were tanners, making goods, saddles, shoes, and belts with leather. They resided at this house at 7219 Ridge Ave. in 1747 and also had a barn on the property, where they manufactured their goods. Because of the Starnes, soldiers from Roxborough during the Revolution all had shoes. The house went into disrepair and was demolished in 1973. (Courtesy of the Philadelphia Historical Commission.)

The Rex family of Germantown was widespread in the area by the time this house, currently at 7515 Ridge Ave., was built in 1805, with several branches of the Rexes nearby, between Wigard and Manatawna Avenues. They were the blacksmiths for the area. This house is still present. (Courtesy of the Philadelphia Historical Commission.)

Capt. Joseph Starne came from a family of tanners, who resided two blocks east of this house, which is currently 7552 Ridge Ave. He joined the Continental Army at age 16 to join his brother at Valley Forge. He became a captain during the War of 1812. He built this stone home in 1795. It later became the estate of Louis Smick. Its roof has been changed since. Today, it remains as a well-maintained house with seven working fireplaces. (Courtesy of Helene Rodgers.)

7552 Ridge Ave. received a new roof, dormer windows, and exterior Colonial wood moldings during the 20th century. This is how the house looks today. (Courtesy of the Philadelphia Historical Commission.)

John Walraven built this house in 1795 at 7558 Ridge Ave. Benjamin Williams, a barrel maker, purchased it in 1803. The Williams family resided at several homes in the area at the time and owned the Williams Store. It has been recently renovated and has three working fireplaces. (Courtesy of the Philadelphia Historical Commission.)

Silhouettes predated photography, and unlike paintings or drawings, they were exacting in producing a person's physical profile. This silhouette is of Benjamin Williams of Roxborough from 1790. (Courtesy of Wesley Cording.)

This 1880 photograph shows the Williams Store at Ridge Avenue and Dearnley Street as it appeared with its porch. It was opened by George Williams in 1825 as a general store and the Roxborough Post Office, though the building dates to 1797. (Courtesy of Crystal Nardone.)

This 1961 photograph shows the old Williams Store at 7568 Ridge Ave. after its porch was removed during the widening of Ridge Avenue. This is fairly close to how the building looks today as a popular deli and sandwich shop. (Courtesy of the Philadelphia Historical Commission.)

The old Buttonball Inn was named for having a buttonball tree in its front yard. It started as the single-family residence of Andrew Crawford in 1764. His son Hugh Crawford, who served in the American Revolution, expanded it into two homes in 1784. Hugh Crawford also opened a stagecoach line from Philadelphia to Reading along with the Buttonball Inn. This building is currently under renovation. (Courtesy of the Philadelphia Historical Commission.)

This small Federal-style house at 7701 Ridge Ave. was built in 1790 and is currently owned in conjunction with a hair salon next door. Interestingly, it sits a few feet lower than street level, indicating its presence before sewers were placed under the street. (Courtesy of the Philadelphia Historical Commission.)

Built in 1825, this house at 7707 Ridge Ave. was nearing demolition but is now a well-maintained home. It is one of many in the Wigard Avenue to Shawmont Avenue area, which makes up one of the largest collection of old Wissahickon schist buildings in the city. (Courtesy of the Philadelphia Historical Commission.)

45

Located at 7925 Ridge Ave. and built in 1785, this unusual house has sidelights, which are windows on either side of the door. Had it been preserved, it would have been one-of-a-kind in Roxborough. Like so many Colonial homes in Roxborough, it fell into disrepair and was demolished in 1985. (Courtesy of the Philadelphia Historical Commission.)

At 7953 Ridge Ave., Joseph Ozias built this house in 1803. It features nidged Ashlar stonework, and its interior has ornate Federal-style woodcarvings adorning its mantles. It currently stands out as a well-maintained business building. (Courtesy of the Philadelphia Historical Commission.)

Though the deed to this lovely home at 8144 Ridge Ave. dates to 1795 and shows the name of Capt. David Jones, it is believed that industrialist Valentine Keely built this home in 1844. It is of the Doric-Greek Revival period. Its louvered shutters are also typical of the period. Unfortunately, the catwalk in the center roof has been removed. (Courtesy of the Philadelphia Historical Commission.)

At 8213 and 8215 Ridge Ave., these c. 1700 homes are similar to New England clapboard-over-log style homes. If the easiest and cheapest resource in an area was wood instead of stone, a log house was built. However, with termites prevalent in the area, log homes rarely survived. These homes were demolished in 1970. (Courtesy of the Philadelphia Historical Commission.)

Appearing as a row of three homes at 8225 through 8229 Ridge Ave. was originally the Ship Tavern, located at Ridge Avenue and Ship Lane, in 1760. Taverns were popular along Ridge Avenue, the major thoroughfare to Reading. The ninth milestone that was in front of this building was moved across the street when the tavern was demolished in 1975. (Courtesy of the Philadelphia Historical Commission.)

Henry Bartle built this home at 8232 Ridge Ave. in 1795. The Bartles were famous for bottle making. The house is unusual, with Swedish gambrel roof and nidged Ashlar stonework on its facade. It currently is a well-maintained home, and the ninth milestone sits in front of the house. The milestones were placed along Ridge Avenue in 1760, when the road was rerouted through Norristown. (Courtesy of the Philadelphia Historical Commission.)

First belonging to Thomas Shepard, this general store at 8238–8240 Ridge Ave. was built in 1827. Often, ornamental porches were added to older buildings during the Victorian era, as this one displays. The building was a farmers market, selling much of the local produce up until its demolition in 2001, which was attributed to water and mortar damage. (Courtesy of the Philadelphia Historical Commission.)

Ridge Avenue at Manatawna Avenue in 1949 displays how rural the area was at that time, with farms, woods, and what is known today as green space. Produce and roadside stands were also plentiful in the area. (Courtesy of Elizabeth Johnston.)

Saint Mary's Episcopal Church stands at the high point of Ridge Avenue and Cathedral Road. It boasts an outstanding window by Philadelphia-based stained-glass artisan Nicola D'Ascenzo. Buried beneath the floor of its chapel are Samuel and Charlotte Houston, whose land the church was built on. (Courtesy of the RMWHS.)

An artist's rendition of how Saint Mary's Episcopal Church was to appear is shown here; however, the current structure only partially resembles this drawing. The church's ground breaking was in 1932. The holy eucharist was first celebrated at Saint Mary's on All Saints' Day in 1934. (Courtesy of the RMWHS.)

On George Washington's first trip west through Roxborough, he noted the sturdiness of the area's stone buildings, as he had not seen such buildings in Center City Philadelphia. This house at 8600 Ridge Ave. defines the sturdiness of Roxborough's Colonial homes and the standard design for many Pennsylvania homes today. In 1962, with new home developments in Roxborough and little interest in acquiring such a home, it was demolished. (Courtesy of the Philadelphia Historical Commission.)

Family-operated stores were commonly found every few blocks along Ridge Avenue. Not only did they sell locally grown produce and locally raised meats but they often sold art and crafts from locals as well. This store with a Dutch gambrel roof at 8900 Ridge Ave. was one of several from Colonial times, which disappeared when super stores came about. (Courtesy of the Philadelphia Historical Commission.)

As the farms disappeared in the 20th century, barns deteriorated too, nearing collapse. Fortunately for this c. 1750 barn at 9040 Ridge Ave., it was restored within a townhouse development. Barns are popular today in Pennsylvania for being restored into living space. (Courtesy of the Philadelphia Historical Commission.)

# *Three*

# RAILWAYS AND BRIDGES

In this snowy scene, cars are attempting to navigate the winding path of Lincoln Drive under the Henry Avenue Bridge. On a sunny day, this route could be an adventure with many curves, protected with modest guardrails to prevent cars from sliding into the Wissahickon Creek. The Henry Avenue Bridge was completed in 1932 at a cost of $1.65 million. The design and construction included two subway tunnels above the arches for the never-built Roxborough line. The stone arch bridge dwarfed by the larger bridge is Hermit's Lane. (Courtesy of the RMWHS.)

Looking outbound at Wissahickon Station in 1926, Rochelle Avenue separates the station from the 1893 trolley car barn of the Wissahickon Electric Passenger Railway (on right). Two separate trolley companies served Wissahickon Station, each using a different track gauge. Although the companies merged and standardized the track gauge, the rails were never connected at Wissahickon. (H. Garforth Collection.)

A three-car inbound Philadelphia & Reading Norristown local crosses the 510-foot-long stone arched bridge in 1924. Bridge pier construction started in 1874 by Nolan & Brothers and was completed by 1882 for $375,000. The original 1833 wooden bridge at this site was built by John Young for the Philadelphia, Germantown & Norristown Railroad, which was leased by the Philadelphia and Reading Railroad in 1870. It cost $30,000 and included Town's lattice truss spans. A fire in 1862 destroyed the original bridge, requiring two interim structures. (Courtesy of the Robert Korpa Collection.)

54

In November 1926, Cranes Confectionery Store offered hot dogs and ice cream cones for 5¢ each. This Ridge Avenue Bridge over the Wissahickon Creek was completed in 1890. The tracks in Ridge Avenue allowed electric trolleys to reach Wissahickon on July 1, 1894. Two months later, the horse-car shuttle to Manayunk (Main Street and Green Lane) was replaced with through electric service. The line was designated Route 61 in 1914. (Courtesy of the Harry Garforth Collection.)

Prior to construction of the Ridge Avenue overpass at Wissahickon, this 1926 view shows the inbound station building, freight tracks to serve Woolen Mills along little Cresson Street, and a fairly narrow Ridge Avenue. Ridge Avenue climbed a steep hill from the Wissahickon Falls and then crossed the railroad at grade. Beyond Ridge Avenue, the huge Pencoyd Steel Complex can be seen, which lined both banks of the Schuylkill River from Wissahickon to Manayunk. Many magnificent iron and steel bridges were built here and used throughout the world. (Courtesy of the Frank Weer Collection.)

On September 29, 1926, a Schuylkill Valley Traction car waits at the outbound platform in Wissahickon for a Philadelphia and Reading Railroad train before departing for Rex (now Summit) Avenue. The line ran six miles up Ridge Avenue on double track through the business district of Roxborough. Beyond the business district, single track was used to reach Barren Hill (over Church Road). Rex Avenue was a short turn location. (Courtesy of Harry Garforth Collection.)

On May 3, 1928, Ridge Avenue overpass construction was underway, forcing Ridge Avenue Line cars destined for Wissahickon to terminate adjacent to the 1887 Wissahickon Public Elementary School. To prevent runaway trolleys, derails were installed here and in Manayunk in 1921. These trolleys ran every 15 minutes and took 35 minutes to reach Barren Hill. After construction was completed, this section of Ridge Avenue became Rochelle Avenue. (H. Garforth Collection.)

Looking down the tracks toward Manayunk, the Richard Hey mansion, "Schuylkill View," built in the 1880s, is on the left. Beyond the mansion in this February 1928 view are the Philadelphia Gas Works tanks and the Saint John the Baptist Church. Cresson Street parallels the railroad all the way through Manayunk, with the railroad tracks eventually running down the middle of the street for several blocks. (Courtesy of the Frank Weer Collection.)

Schuylkill View possessed various intricate architectural details. Access to the stone mansion was up staircases and a steep winding driveway from Main Street. Stone walls lined the drive, with benches included for soaking in Schuylkill River scenery in less hectic times. On Main Street, at the base of the drive, was the stone carriage house that survived into the year 2010. The multistory Richard Hey and Sons Woolen Mills fronted on Main Street, adjacent to the mansion. (Courtesy of the Frank Weer/Harry Garforth Collection.)

On March 27, 1930, retaining wall form work is progressing at a feverish pace along Cresson Street, between Jamestown (formerly Cedar Street) and Pensdale Streets. The rear of the ornate buildings of Saint John the Baptist Church and School can be seen in the distance. The design of the church is based on a cathedral located in France. Trains are continuing to operate during the construction over a single track now elevated on the inbound side. (Courtesy of the Frank Weer Collection.)

Looking outbound at the Manayunk Station, one sees the Frank Furness–inspired design with flared chimneys and varying roof angles. A crowd has gathered next to the outbound platform, perhaps picking up the latest news. Long trains destined for points west, such as Norristown, Pottstown, and Reading, stopped here, blocking the numerous street crossings while passengers, mail, and baggage were handled. (Courtesy of phillyhistory.org, a project of the Philadelphia Department of Records.)

On March 14, 1930, an inbound train stops at the old street-level platform in Manayunk, just short of Levering Street. The project to elevate the railroad required intense coordination between the railroad and its contractors in the late 1920s and early 1930s. The Reading Railroad project to electrify its suburban commuter lines was well underway by this time. The Norristown Branch electrification was deferred until grade crossing elimination projects along the line were completed. Electric train operation to Norristown commenced on January 30, 1933. (Courtesy of the Bruce Saylor Collection.)

In 1930, the Great Atlantic and Pacific store on the right contrasts sharply with today's big box stores. A ramp allows access to the new outbound Manayunk station and platform. The station included elevators to move baggage from street level up to both platforms. The outbound station building serves as a banquet hall today. Although no off-street parking exists, hundreds of SEPTA commuters use the station today, walking from the dense housing surrounding the station. (Frank Weer Collection.)

Looking inbound on February 28, 1928, one can appreciate the Frank Furness–designed features of the crossing shanty roof and the main Manayunk Station Building built in 1887. Eight street crossings required protection when trains operated through Manayunk. Manpower operated the gates at each crossing. In 1928, a total of 33 daily Reading Railroad trains passed through Manayunk. After electrified operation commenced on January 30, 1933, the train count increased to 58. (Courtesy of Hagley Museum.)

This January 3, 1928, view is looking toward Belmont Hills across both the old and new Green Lane Bridges over the Schuylkill River. Green Lane originally crossed the Reading Railroad at grade and ducked under the Pennsylvania Railroad. PRR concrete arch bridge #7.70, built in 1917, replaced the original "S" Bridge constructed in 1884. Upon completion of the Reading Railroad elevation over Cresson Street, green Lane was dug out to pass beneath the railroad. The Smartley and Son office (builders and coal dealer) is to the left. (Courtesy of the Frank Weer Collection.)

Looking down from the Pennsylvania Railroad Manayunk Station on March 4, 1930, the new Reading Company freight station and the recently completed 1928 Green Lane Bridge are visible. The large PRR Bridge replaced the original "S" Bridge in 1917. Newly installed electric catenary structures for PRR Norristown service are evident on the bridge. Electric passenger trains ran across the bridge from 1930 until 1986, when deteriorated conditions forced service to end at Cynwyd. Two hundred and fifty passengers continue to use the remaining three stations of this once 90-mile line. (Frank Weer Collection.)

On Main Street looking toward Green Lane, four Route 61 trolleys are stopped. The double-ended cars are queued up to cross over to the inbound rail during the retaining wall construction. When the construction is completed, a wye track will be installed to turn the trolleys. Route 61 began operation between Green Lane and Leverington Avenue on October 25, 1909. (H. Garforth Collection.)

Route 61 provided direct service from Manayunk to Philadelphia's commercial district along Market Street. Strawbridge and Clothier, Gimbel Brothers, and Lit Brothers all had multilevel stores stretching for full city blocks. Trolleys travelled all the way down Ridge Avenue to loop on Eighth, Walnut, and Ninth Streets. Trolleys ran until 1941, yielding to trackless trolleys. On the Manayunk end, after 1930, Route 61 trolleys turned on an unusual wye located in the intersection of Main Street and Leverington Avenue. (Courtesy of the Harry Garforth Collection.)

In January 1907, a passenger car follows a snow sweeper, while workers dig out the deep snow ahead. Both cars have just passed Fountain Street and are working their way west toward Lemont Street on Ridge Avenue. Trolleys operated both ways on a single track west of Fairthorne Street, with passing sidings located near Wigard and Summit Avenues. The sidings allowed opposing trolley movements to pass. (Courtesy of the RMWHS.)

The bridging of the Schuylkill River at Green Lane and Belmont Avenue dates back to 1833. The iron bridge shown here was constructed in 1864. The narrow two-lane structure lasted until 1928, when a new concrete bridge was installed adjacent to the older bridge, allowing traffic to be maintained during construction. The 1928 closed spandrel arch structure stretched 564 feet. (Courtesy of phillyhistory.org, a project of the Philadelphia Department of Records.)

Here is one of several bridges along the "Forbidden Drive" crossing the Wissahickon Creek, connecting the Roxborough and Andorra communities to Chestnut Hill, Mount Airy, and Germantown. Most of the bridges were originally covered bridges and were replaced later with stone bridges. Of the 126 stone arch bridges in the greater Philadelphia area, five were located in the Wissahickon Valley. (Courtesy of the RMWHS.)

School children attend the opening of the Walnut Lane Bridge in 1908 in their Sunday best. Over 1,000 revelers joined the dedication. (Courtesy of phillyhistory.org, a project of the Philadelphia Department of Records.)

To support the World War II effort, Route 61 trolley rails on Main Street are being reclaimed for war use. Pencoyd Iron and Steel Works was to the left, allowing for quick use of the extracted rails. (Courtesy of Temple University Libraries, Urban Archives/ Philadelphia, Pennsylvania.)

# *Four*

# OUR COMMUNITY

Pictured here is Howard
Williams. He operated the
trolley for many years at the
Parker Avenue switch of
the Ridge Avenue Trolley.
(Courtesy of Wesley Cording.)

The Roxborough Home for Women welcomed occupants in 1887, making it the oldest gerontology center for women in America. It was previously named the Gorgas Home for Women after its benefactors. Susan Gorgas had given a generous gift that enabled the construction of a new building. Furness, Evans & Company designed the structure. (Courtesy of Hilma Larkin.)

To start off the 1924 Buddy Poppy Drive to provide for disabled and needy veterans, Ruth Knipe is decorating George W. Gillett, a Grand Army veteran, with a Buddy Poppy. Thomas H.A. Turner, the commander of the Hattal-Taylor Post 333, assists her. The organization's name honors the first member of the community to fall on the battlefields of Europe in World War I. (Courtesy of Hattal-Taylor, Post 333, Veterans of Foreign Wars.)

Roxborough High School played against Saint John the Baptist of Manayunk every Thanksgiving, as seen here in 1932. (Courtesy of the RMWHS.)

Women of the Lutheran Archives are shown in line, ready to run the various organizations of the church. Grace Lutheran Church had ties to many Roxborough community events in the early 20th century. (Courtesy of the Lutheran Archives Center.)

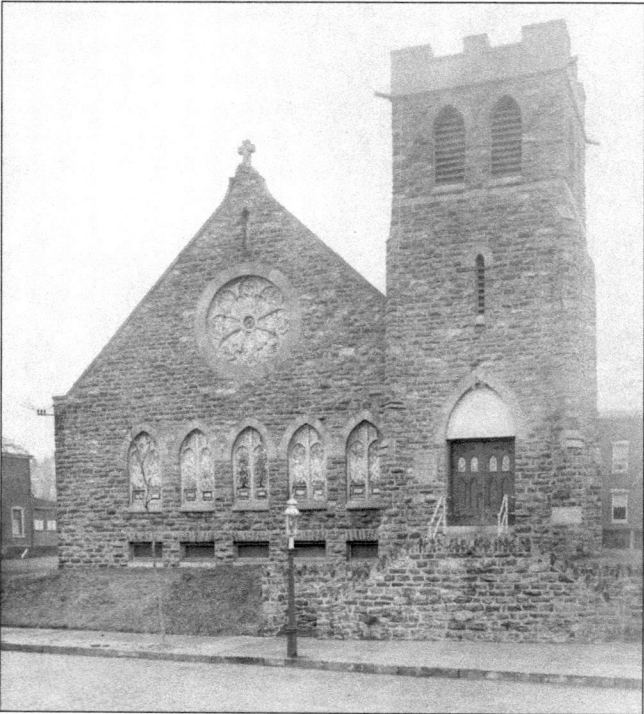

Grace Lutheran, seen here, was built after the early Wood estate was demolished. It was recently purchased for new real estate development, as has been the case with many old building sites in Roxborough. (Courtesy of Wanda O. Rehder.)

School children are pictured in one of the many programs run by the church, which ranged from parades to plays. (Courtesy of the Philadelphia Lutheran Archives Center.)

Francis Speight is seen here painting local scenes in and around Roxborough, where much hidden beauty awaits an artist's brush. (Courtesy of the Southern Historical Collection, Wilson Library, University of North Carolina at Chapel Hill.)

Gorgas Park, pictured in the 1950s, was and still is a popular green space for community gatherings in Roxborough. For 80 years, public events have filled the summer weekends here, in addition to observances by the 21st Ward Veterans on Memorial Day, Veterans Day, and Pearl Harbor Day. (Courtesy of Temple University Libraries, Urban Archives, Philadelphia, Pennsylvania.)

Meyer Guggenheim and his wife, Barbara, raised seven boys in this house at Green Lane and Mitchell Street in Roxborough. Their son Benjamin was lost in the *Titanic* sinking in 1912. (Courtesy of the RMWHS.)

The yard at Saint Timothy's Episcopal Church on Ridge Avenue is a beautiful setting. Here is Reverend Dennison reading the Bible nearly a century ago. Even today, Saint Timothy's stands out as an unusual, eye-catching structure. (Courtesy of Saint Timothy's Episcopal Church.)

This seal, designed by William B. Forney Jr. in 1940, was officially adopted as the symbol for the Roxborough 250th anniversary celebration. The laurel border honors those men who have defined the nation; the turtle represents the Lenni Lenape who made their home here; the oak tree stood in front of Hattal-Taylor Post VFW; the watermark is that of William Rittenhouse's paper mill and the symbol used by the Pietists, the first religious sect to the area. In 2009, the Philadelphia Mural Arts Program along with the Roxborough Development Corporation sponsored a project with mural artist Dennis Haugh. After meeting with interested community members and the Roxborough, Manayunk, and Wissahickon Historical Society, the turtle was chosen symbolizing the Lenni Lenape myth of creation. Located at Ridge Avenue and Conarroe Street, the turtle shell pattern depicts a map of the streets of Roxborough surrounded by hilly green spaces. (Courtesy of the RMWHS.)

James Schofield (seated, back left) followed in his father's footsteps by becoming the manager of Dobson's Mills in 1900. (Courtesy of Crystal Nardone.)

This vehicle advertises the 1926 Sesquitennial that was held in South Philadelphia. Plans to hold the massive event in Roxborough were not approved. (Courtesy of Temple University Libraries, Urban Archives, Philadelphia, Pennsylvania.)

The community's only high school, Roxborough High School, is the only school in Philadelphia that houses the middle and high schools together. It is seen in this photograph taken after World War II; during wartime, 1,600 Roxborough graduates fought in that war, and 97 were killed. (Courtesy of Temple University Libraries, Urban Archives, Philadelphia, Pennsylvania.)

This picture from Immaculate Heart of Mary Roman Catholic Church shows first graders preparing to receive their First Holy Communion in 1955. (Courtesy of Father Paul O'Brimski.)

"Renew your home—restore prosperity" was the slogan used in the Renovize Philadelphia Campaign in 1932, which encouraged property owners to pledge for home and business improvements, repairs, and modernization by contracting local skilled artisans as an effective means to relieve unemployment at the time. Griffith Yarnell was in business for over 50 years. (Courtesy of Judith Koval.)

RIDGE AVENUE M. E. CHURCH AND PARSONAGE, ROXBOROUGH

Ridge Avenue Methodist Church and its rectory currently stand at Ridge and Shawmont Avenues. Organized in 1847, the church was enlarged in 1871. Today, it hosts many community events. (Courtesy of the RMWHS.)

Posing on Lyceum Avenue, the newly chartered VFW post gets ready to march in Roxborough. The organization's bands marched until the mid-1970s. Currently, Post 333 has a membership of 190 veterans. (Courtesy of Hattal-Taylor, Post 333.)

Pencoyd workers pose for this 1880 photograph. Pencoyd Iron Works employed 6,000 people at the turn of the 20th century. (Courtesy of the RMWHS.)

Awarded a citation for gallantry in action while stationed on a destroyer undergoing aerial attack, Harold Edward Howley served in the Marine Corps in World War II in the South Pacific. He returned from the war and opened Howley's Market and coached the Biddy (youth sports) basketball team in Roxborough. (Courtesy of Donna Howley.)

Francis "Babe" Gagliano (first row, far right) was acclaimed to be one of the best shortstops in Philadelphia. Shown in this photograph, the 21st Ward semiprofessional baseball team played against the best sandlot teams in the city, attracting fans by the thousands. Teams played in and around Roxborough at several popular fields: RoxyAA, "Dego Louie's," Pencoyd Field, Clifford Park, Roxborough High School field, and the Blue Socks/Hawk's field. The Wissahickon Hawks, a semiprofessional football team, put Roxborough on the map in the 1940s through the 1960s. (Courtesy of Frank Gagliano.)

In 1934, Roxborough High School's basketball team had a strong group of players, including Alfred McNally (second row, far left), and Harold Howley (second row, third from left). (Courtesy of Donna Howley.)

In this 1957 photograph, in their first season, are the Wissahickon Civic Association Braves, one of the four charter baseball teams in the 21st Ward Junior Baseball League. Started by Francis "Babe" Gagliano, 60 boys participated the first year, 15 on each team, playing at Daisy Field. In 2006, celebrating 50 years, the 21st Ward Baseball and Softball Leagues numbered approximately 800 boys and girls playing at the Al Perlman Sports Complex. (Courtesy of Frank Gagliano.)

Pictured are John Hagenbucher Sr. (left) and his son John Jr. John Sr. served in the Civil War and, having been wounded three times, returned to Roxborough and worked in Robert's Mill and built houses. John Jr. was a superintendent at Pencoyd Iron and Steel Works. They resided at their Freeland Avenue home, pictured here. (Courtesy of Doris Hagenbucher.)

HORSE SHOW

under the auspices of the

ROXBOROUGH RIDING CLUB

For the Benefit of the MEMORIAL HOSPITAL OF ROXBOROUGH

Saturday, May 23rd, 1931     11 A. M. to 6 P. M.

JUMPING JACK FARMS

Manatawna Avenue, East of Ridge Avenue, Roxborough, Phila.

PRICE    ::    10c

Situated on the edge of the Wissahickon Valley, equestrian activity in Roxborough and surrounding areas prevailed, and both private and public riding stables could be found in several Roxborough locations. Jumping Jack Farms, located where the Andorra Playing Fields are now, provided facilities for the Roxborough Riding Club's benefit shows, as well as pasture areas for horses from nearby Carpenter Lane Stable. (Courtesy of the RMWHS.)

Stanley Cauffman started the Wissahickon Historical Society and played cello for the Philadelphia Orchestra. He was also a founding member of the Roxborough Symphony Orchestra. (Courtesy of Jo Cauffman.)

Members of the Merrick family started the Roxborough Hospital by donating their home, Evergreens, as a place to heal the sick with seven beds. The current Roxborough Memorial Hospital was built on this site. (Courtesy of RMWHS.)

Currently at Ridge Avenue and Vassar Street and used by the Northern Home for Children, is the Saint Timothy's Workingmen's Club and Institute, built in 1877. It served as a center for education and recreation for working men in the Wissahickon community. (Courtesy of Saint Timothy's Episcopal Church.)

Roxborough residents have enjoyed the pool at the Kendrick Recreation Center, known affectionately as the "Bathey," for decades. In the 1930s, as seen here, swimming was not co-ed. (Courtesy of Donna Howley.)

Saint Timothy's Hospital and House of Mercy's ambulance was reliable, though a bit bumpy. (Courtesy of the RMWHS.)

Memorial Hospital in Roxborough staffed 300 people in 1950. Ambulances at the time were extended station wagons. (Courtesy of RMWHS.)

The Wm. M. Keely & Son milk truck filled residents' bottles with milk. Milk bottles were filled on request from a small tank, as pictured here. (Courtesy of RMWHS.)

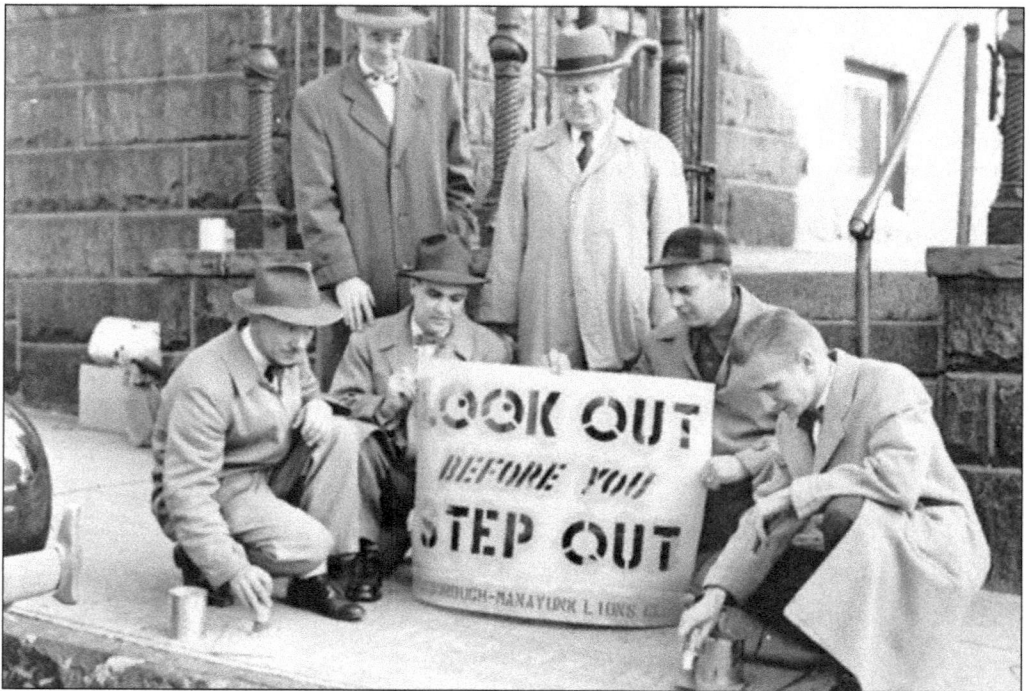

The Roxborough-Manayunk Lion's Club sponsored sidewalk improvements in front of North Light Community Center. (Courtesy of RMWHS.)

Nicholas "Nick" and Sylvia Myers have dedicated much time and effort to discovering and preserving local history. Before Nick passed away, they were frequently seen at the Roxborough Branch Library together and were active members in numerous community organizations. (Courtesy of Lisa Myers.)

The flute club of Levering School in 1936 was an all-grade group. Brothers James (second grade: front row, far left) and William (sixth grade: third row, second from left) played in the band. (Courtesy of James Barnes.)

German immigrants Adam Fair and wife Susanne married in 1882 raising seven children. Pictured here are Harry, Floss, Liz, Levi and baby Laura. Laura Fair Howley lived to be 105-years old living on Lauriston Street most of her life. (Courtesy of Donna Howley.)

Josephine Zingaro immigrated to America with her parents from Italy as a young teen and raised four children with husband, Domenic, a railroad worker. A self-made businesswoman, she leased properties, including a string of Umbria Street garages, and raised rabbits for sale. In the 1920s, she posed with her niece Emma Santoro and—proud of her literacy—a book. Several descendents live in Roxborough today. (Courtesy of Kathleen Zingaro.)

American-born Mary DeSantis donned the traditional garb of her parents' home country, Italy, for a local parade around 1917. She and Michael Zingaro purportedly eloped as teenagers but were kept apart by parents until "officially" wed by a priest from Saint Lucy. Happily married 65 years, they raised five children, all attendees of Roxborough High School and, later, hosted regular Sunday dinners for an expanded family that included spouses and 15 grandchildren. (Courtesy of Kathleen Zingaro.)

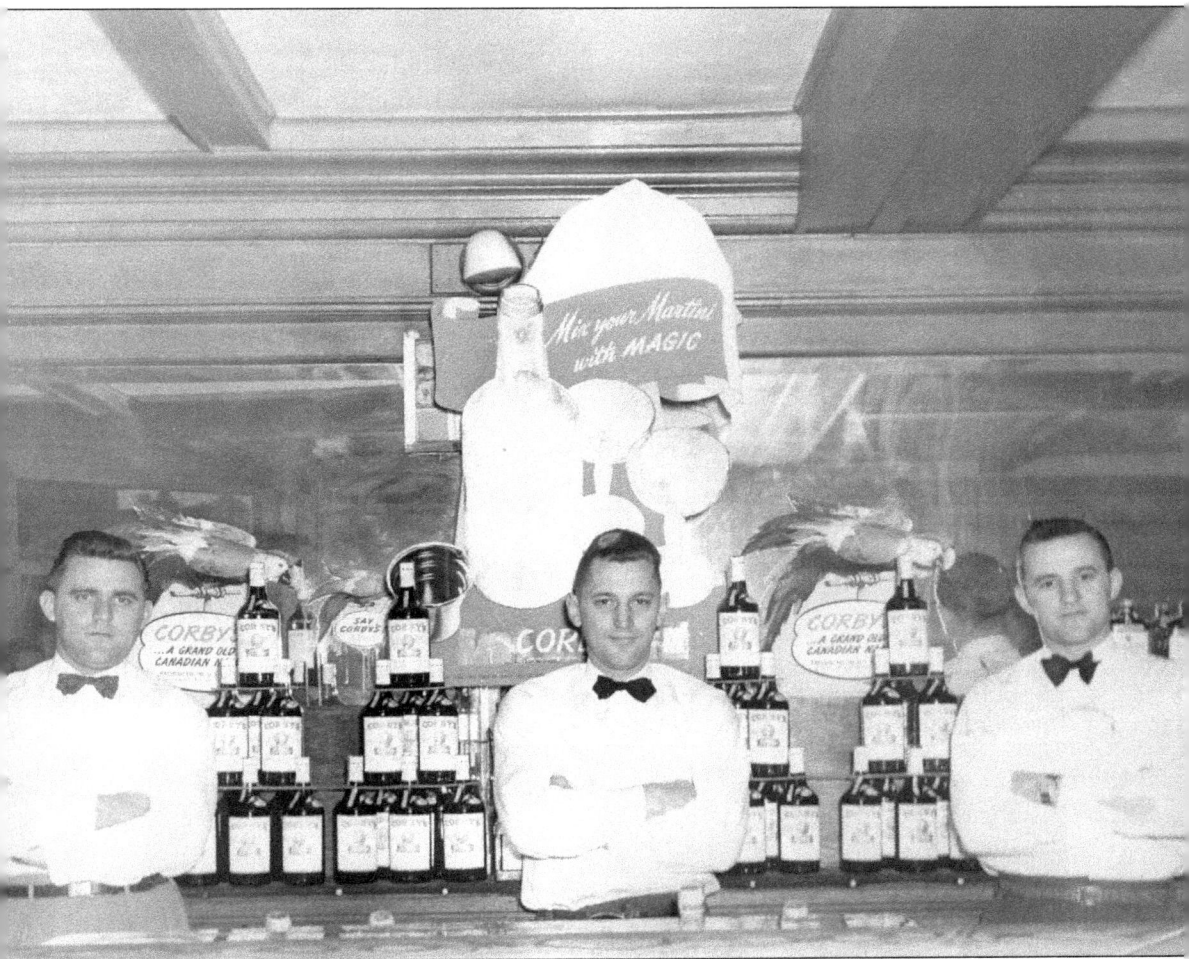

From left to right, bartenders Walt Konapka, Chops Stanzak, and Gene Konapka pose smartly for this photograph in 1947 in what was then known as the K&S Bar. Today, Coyle's Café is a popular watering hole for thirsty and hungry Roxboroughians. (Courtesy of the Coyle family.)

Charles Lindbergh promoted gliding as the "new sport" in the 1920s. Roxborough was well suited for gliding because of its altitude and open spaces. Here a young gentleman is pictured in his "motorless craft" southwest of Ridge Avenue. (Courtesy of Irene Madrak.)

John Anderson, seated on his glider at age 19, was the first member of the Roxborough Glider Club to glide. He built a glider at the Kendrick Recreation Center at Ridge and Roxborough Avenues. (Courtesy of Irene Madrak.)

## Five

# I LOVE A PARADE

For Canal Day in Manayunk in 1997, the Roxborough, Manayunk, and Wissahickon Historical Society proudly walks the banner. Pictured are Nicholas Myers (left), David Henderson (right), and Vincent Hillanbrand and son. Samuel Lawson started the Fourth of July parade tradition in 1831. (Courtesy of the RMWHS.)

Memorial Day parades, such as this one following World War I, were popular in Philadelphia. Memorial ceremonies were commonly held in Leverington Cemetery, which is where the people seen here were on the path to. (Courtesy of Wanda O. Rehder.)

In front of the VFW, Morris Hunter, a decorated war veteran, holds the flag. (Courtesy of Hattal-Taylor, Post 333, Veterans of Foreign Wars.)

A military procession during a Memorial Day parade depicts young men during the 1920s celebrating the Allied victory in World War I. (Courtesy of the RMWHS.)

Pictured during the 1920s is a Memorial Day parade on its way to conduct a ceremony at the World War I memorial at Gorgas Park after leaving a ceremony at Leverington Cemetery. (Courtesy of the RMWHS.)

Fourth of July parades have always been popular in Roxborough, as seen here during the 1950s. A celebration followed at Gorgas Park, often with fireworks. (Courtesy of the RMWHS.)

During a Fourth of July parade, a sign honoring "the oldest living member, Miss M. Geary," was hung from the side of a 1951 Ford convertible, which not only dates the picture but also indicates the regard for the community's elderly at the time. (Courtesy of the RMWHS.)

Pictured during the 1940s is a Fourth of July parade, with its musicians at Ridge and Lyceum Avenues. To the left is the Odd Fellows Hall, built during the 1880s and demolished a few years after this photograph was taken. (Courtesy of the RMWHS.)

Patriotism has always been popular in Roxborough as depicted by this guard and their flags, serving their state and country. During the American Revolution, over 90 men from Roxborough marched to Valley Forge. (Courtesy of the RMWHS.)

Pictured is a Fourth of July parade during the 1920s on Lyceum Avenue near Ridge Avenue, where many businesses were located at the south end of the Roxborough business district. (Courtesy of the RMWHS.)

An elaborate Fourth of July parade during the Sesquicentennial celebration in 1926 is pictured along Ridge Avenue. Costumes accompanied scenes of colonial times depicting the American Revolution. (Courtesy of the RMWHS.)

Civil War veterans march on Lyceum Avenue in the 1920s accompanied by the Wissahickon trolley. (Courtesy of RMWHS.)

Tin cups for lemonade were a popular Fourth of July tradition in Roxborough as souveniers holding memories. (Courtesy of Temple University Libraries, Urban Archives, Philadelphia, Pennsylvania.)

# Six

# THE FRINGE

These are the Monastery Stables, which were built along with the Dunkard Monastery along Kitchen's Lane in 1745. The stables are still in use. (Courtesy of John Johnstone.)

Built in 1745, this monastery on Kitchen's Lane was inhabited by a group of monks known as the Dunkards, who branched off from the Mennonites. They performed full-body baptisms in the Wissahickon Creek and had ties to other Dunkards at the time in Ephrata. The Dunkards today have churches in Pennsylvania. (Courtesy of John Johnstone.)

The small attic window near the front of this house at 225 Port Royal Ave. represents the original section of a three-room, three-story house dating to 1720. It was originally the Barr farm and is currently the oldest house on Port Royal Avenue. Port Royal Avenue was the original route used by soldiers who were encamped in Roxborough and had to trek to Valley Forge. (Courtesy of John Johnstone.)

Horse-and-carriage rentals were common into the early 20th century, as they were the main source of transporting goods and people along roadways. Just about every town had such rentals. This large, c. 1789 stable stood at 641 Shawmont Ave. and was demolished in the early 1960s. (Courtesy of the Philadelphia Historical Commission.)

Little houses add character to a neighborhood, amidst the large, cookie-cutter construction that is so common today. This c. 1800 house still proudly stands at 623 Shawmont Ave., sitting below street level. This was because sewers were put in place after the house was constructed. (Courtesy of the Philadelphia Historical Commission.)

Rockshade, located in the 100 block of Parker Avenue, was a summer tavern dating to the 1850s. Architecturally, it was very similar to the Indian Rock Hotel, which stood along Forbidden Drive in Wissahickon Park. (Courtesy of the Philadelphia Historical Commission.)

Along the Schuylkill River, bordering current Manayunk, there was the small village of Cinnaminson, consisting mostly of an early Swedish settlement. This house and barn combination, dating to 1660 at 301 Parker Ave., was a log building covered with cement. This structure enabled the owner to tend to animals during winter months without enduring the elements. Likely, this house did not have windows initially, but only tightly closing shutters to keep out the elements. This house was demolished in 1980. (Courtesy of the Philadelphia Historical Commission.)

Green Lane, as it leaves Manayunk and ascends into Roxborough, contains beautiful specimens of architecture, including homes from the late part of the Federal era to more ornate and massive Victorian homes. At 358 Green Lane, this c. 1830 home is the oldest remaining one on that road. (Courtesy of the Philadelphia Historical Commission.)

At 460 Green Lane is this c. 1840 Federal home with a complete set of original shutters. During the industrial peak of Manayunk, mill owners, physicians, and lawyers built their homes at "the top of the hill," while mill workers lived in row houses nearer to the mills in Manayunk. (Courtesy of the Philadelphia Historical Commission.)

THE DEVIL'S POOL, WISSAKICKON CREEK,
PHILADELPHIA, PA.

*from S. & W.*

1896   ILLUSTRATED POST CARD CO., N. Y.

Near the mouth of Cresheim Creek is Devil's Pool. A rustic bridge leads over the gorge at the mouth of the creek, near the spot where it empties into the Wissahickon. Many believe the legend that this was a place of Native American worship, where the good and evil spirits fought each other. (Courtesy of Valerie James.)

Wissahicken Creek, at Lover's Leap, Fairmount Park, Philadelphia, Pa.

Here, so the legend goes, the daughter of a mighty Indian chief and her young lover plunged to their deaths in these waters. The rock is known as Lover's Leap. (Courtesy of Valerie James.)

Looking up the hill on the left is believed to be the barn on the property that was once owned by Daniel and Phoebe Righter. On the right is Lauriston cottage, currently an ongoing excavation project headed by Temple University and the Kelpius Society. (Courtesy of the *Episcopal Register*.)

Seen here around 1905, this is the cave at Gorgas Lane and Forbidden Drive. It was the site of the Roxborough Mining Company, which operated in 1763–1764, leasing five acres from Jacob Livezey. During the American Revolution, provisions were hidden in the cave, which was later closed up. Horatio Gates Jones rediscovered the cave in 1854. (Courtesy of Donald S. Sloan.)

Sometimes hidden in its little glen, but usually visible from Forbidden Drive, is the Livezey house, built in sections between 1685 and 1745. It was also the former home of the Valley Green Canoe Club. Note the spring house in the upper right corner of the postcard. (Courtesy of Valerie James.)

Bucolic scenes like this on the Wissahickon Creek are reminiscent of simpler times. (Courtesy of Eric Sabaroff / Valley Green Canoe Club.)

Courting and canoeing on the Wissahickon in their Sunday best was a favorite pastime of many local residents. (Courtesy of Eric Sabaoff.)

MEMORIAL DAY - 1928

Canoeing on the Wissahickon Creek has been a popular sport for decades. (Courtesy of Eric Sabaroff / Valley Green Canoe Club.)

This photograph illustrates the solitude on the creek. (Courtesy of Eric Sabaroff.)

Pictured in 1910 is a happy crowd gathered for an outing at the Livezy house. (Courtesy of Eric Sabaroff / Valley Green Canoe Club.)

Workers chop off blocks of ice in the frozen Wissahickon and load them on wagons to sell to local icehouses. These blocks of ice served as early refrigeration. (Courtesy of Donald S. Sloan.)

The steps of Manayunk, called the "100s," helped residents travel from Manayunk to Roxborough by foot. There are 13 sets of stairs totaling 1,300 steps. (Courtesy of Hilma Larkin.)

The City of Philadelphia decided to filter its water supply by building five sand filtration plants; two of these were in Roxborough. This photograph shows the leveling of the ground, near the present Eva and Dearnley Streets, for the Lower Roxborough Filter Plant. In the early 20th century, most of this work was still done by hand and horsepower. (Courtesy of the Philadelphia Water Department.)

This large reservoir, part of Philadelphia's drinking water supply, seen in 1897, is still located along Port Royal Avenue and Lare Street. While it was drained for repairs, crews of men worked to remove the mud and coal dust that settled out of the river water. Until sand filtrations were built to purify the polluted river water, this settlement was the only treatment the water received. (Courtesy of the Philadelphia Water Department.)

The large drinking water purification filters in Roxborough were the first in the city to go into service. This picture is with the sand in place but before the water was added to the filters. Basically, polluted river water flowed through the sand, which trapped impurities. Pipes below the sand collected the purified water, which was then stored in reservoirs and distributed to homes and businesses by a network of pipes. (Courtesy of the Philadelphia Water Department.)

# ABOUT THE ORGANIZATION

The Roxborough, Manayunk, and Wissahickon Historical Society was formed when the *Suburban Press* newspaper printed an article about the Jacob Cook house in 1967.

The house was built in 1747 on the property currently occupied by the YMCA at Ridge Avenue and Domino Lane. Attempts were made to save this local historical landmark through the intervention of the 21st Ward Community Council. The council's president at the time, Paul Clymer, appointed Claire Kelly to head a historical committee, thus beginning the formation of RMWHS with Fred Turner as the first president.

The society is dedicated to the advancement of historical information though education, collections, and presentation of artifacts, photographs, and memorabilia related to Roxborough, Manayunk, Wissahickon, and surrounding communities as caretakers of the area's rich history for future generations.

Through a firm commitment by our members, I am hopeful our society will continue to flourish and effectively serve our community by preserving its treasured past.

—Donald S. Sloan, president

Visit us at
arcadiapublishing.com

www.ingramcontent.com/pod-product-compliance
Lightning Source LLC
Chambersburg PA
CBHW050547110426
42813CB00008B/2281